Pa

MW01222863

The 400

Sue Leather

Series Editors:
Rob Waring and Sue Leather
Series Story Consultant: Julian Thomlinson
Story Editor: Julian Thomlinson

NATIONAL
GEOGRAPHIC
LEARNING

CENGAGE
Learning·

Australia • Brazil • Japan • Korea • Mexico • Singapore • Spain • United Kingdom • United States

Page Turners Reading Library
The 400
Sue Leather

Publisher: Andrew Robinson

Executive Editor: Sean Bermingham

Editorial Assistant: Dylan Mitchell

Director of Global Marketing:
Ian Martin

Senior Content Project Manager:
Tan Jin Hock

Manufacturing Planner:
Mary Beth Hennebury

Contributors:
Vessela Gasper, Jessie Chew

Layout Design and Illustrations:
Redbean Design Pte Ltd

Cover Illustration: Eric Foenander

Photo Credits:
52 Evlakhov Valeriy/Shutterstock

ISBN-13: 978-1-4240-1843-7

ISBN-10: 1-4240-1843-9

National Geographic Learning
20 Channel Center Street
Boston, Massachusetts 02210
USA

Cengage Learning is a leading provider of customized learning solutions with office locations around the globe, including Singapore, the United Kingdom, Australia, Mexico, Brazil, and Japan. Locate your local office at:
international.cengage.com/region

Cengage Learning products are represented in Canada by Nelson Education, Ltd.

Visit National Geographic Learning online at
NGL.Cengage.com

Visit our corporate website at
www.cengage.com

Printed in the United States of America
1 2 3 4 5 6 7 – 18 17 16 15 14

Contents

Review

Background Reading

People in the story

Kat Gupta
an eighteen-year-old
400-meter runner

Salma Imran
Kat's friend

Tara Patel
Kat's rival, a 400-meter runner

Gina Martin
an 800-meter runner

Coach Jeff Cox
Kat's coach at Kingston Harriers,
an athletic club in London

The story is set in London, England.

Chapter 1

A new club

"Come on, everyone!" said Coach Cox. "Take a short break and then try that start again."

Kat Gupta held her sides and breathed hard. Wasn't it time to stop yet? It seemed like hours. First, there was the warm-up, then lots of exercises in the gym to make their legs stronger. Finally, she had to run four kilometers on the club track. Her legs hurt, and she felt like she couldn't breathe.

"It's only three months to the Nationals," the coach added.

I have to get faster, thought Kat. She'd been at her new club, Kingston Harriers, for two weeks now, and she was still more than a full second slower than Tara Patel, who was the slowest of the other four 400-meter runners. And, as the coach said, the National Championships were only three months away!

Everyone said that Kingston Harriers was the best athletic club in the country, and Kat was happy to be training with the first team. It was a great chance for her to compete at the National Championships. Getting to the Nationals was Kat's dream and it was a first step toward running for Great Britain. But every training session here was twice as long as the training at her old club. It was nine o'clock in the evening now, and she still had to take a bus and then the Tube to get home across London.

Kat looked across at Tara and the other 400-meter runners. They were talking and laughing together. They didn't look tired at all. The club was the strongest in the country for the 400, and the top four runners in Britain were here.

They were practicing running the first hundred meters. Kat ran again, but she wasn't able to run any faster. In fact, she was slower. She tried hard, but she felt tired.

Jeff Cox looked at her. "OK, Kat," he said. "You can stop there for this evening. Have a good rest, and think about everything you've learned."

On the bus, Kat looked out the window at the dark London night and thought. Each athletic club in England could send four female 400-meter runners to the National Championships. How could she, Kat, get onto the Kingston Harriers team? The others were really fast and confident. Could she possibly beat Tara Patel's time in the three months before the Nationals?

"Well, of course it isn't going to be easy," Kat's best friend Salma told her a few days later. "But you always knew that."

"I know, Salma, I know that," Kat said. "It's just that when I look at those other runners there I ask myself . . ."

"What?"

"Well, you know, if I'm as good as they are . . ." Kat said quietly.

The two of them were in Salma's room, listening to music and talking as they often did. Salma was sitting on her bed, Kat across the room on a big comfortable chair.

7

Kat didn't have any brothers or sisters, and Salma was almost like a sister to her. She knew Salma's mother and father, and her older brother, Moin. Salma knew Kat's parents, too. Kat and Salma had been at the same schools all their lives, and now they were both in the first year at their local college, where Salma studied History and Kat studied Sports Science. Salma was really the only person she could talk to about her doubts.

"Kat Gupta!" Salma almost shouted. "Good? You know you're a champion! You've always been a champion! Remember when you won the London Juniors when you were ten? Are you crazy? I won't let you talk like that!"

Kat smiled. Dear Salma!

"Winning Junior Championships is one thing, Salma," she said. "But now I'm eighteen, I'm an adult. Things are much more difficult. There's more competition."

"Well, yes, I know it's different. But that's why you joined Kingston, isn't it?"

"Yes, I know you're right," Kat said. "I just wish you were with me at the club, I guess. I wish I had a friend there." She missed Salma now that she was at Kingston Harriers. She didn't have much time to see her friend because her training took so much time. At college, they studied different subjects, so they didn't see each other much.

"Just keep on working hard," Salma said, as they said goodbye. "You'll do well. You know you will. You know how to work hard."

"Yeah, I suppose I do," Kat said.

Salma smiled and added, "Not like me!"

Kat laughed at her friend. "I'm a bit lazy, I suppose," Salma often said about herself. It wasn't true, as Kat knew. Salma worked hard at things she really loved, like History.

Just then there was a knock on the door.

"Who is it?" asked Salma.

The door opened and Moin, Salma's older brother, put his head around it.

"Hey, Kat," said Moin. "I just came to say hello. How're things going?"

"Hi, Moin," Kat smiled. "How are you? How's work?"

Moin came in and sat down at Salma's desk. "Oh, OK, I suppose." Moin worked at a local pharmacy. "What about you, though? Salma tells me you've changed clubs."

Kat told him all about it.

"It sounds like you're all alone," he said. "What about the other girls or guys at the club? Is there anyone nice?"

"I don't know really," Kat said. She didn't have any friends at the club, she told them. The other 400-meter runners like Tara Patel were competitors for places in the Nationals. Because only four girls could go to the Nationals, the others weren't very friendly to her. She didn't know anyone else yet.

Salma suddenly jumped up from her bed and said, "Mum's made some chicken curry. I can smell it from here. You'd better eat a lot now before you get into all that hard training. Come on, Kat, I'll race you downstairs."

"I don't know if I've got the energy," Kat said.

Chapter 2

A new friend

Kat worked as hard as ever in the next training session. But she still wasn't as good as the other girls. In the gym, she felt the others were stronger than her. On the track, she was running well in the training races, but she was still far slower than the others.

Come on, Kat, she said to herself. She tried to make a picture in her mind of herself running for Great Britain, coming in first and winning a gold medal. That was how she usually made herself work. But somehow it didn't help her now. She tried hard, but when she looked at the others, she just didn't feel great. At the end of the training session, Coach Cox said to the runners, "OK, everyone, go and change. Kat, come here please."

Kat walked over to the coach.

"What's the matter, Kat?" he asked.

"Nothing," she said, trying to smile.

"It doesn't look like nothing."

"I don't know . . . I'm just a bit frustrated," she said. "I expect to be getting closer to the others, but I'm not."

"Well, it takes time," said the coach.

"Hmm." Kat looked down.

"Listen, Kat. I know you can do it," he said. "What about your start? That will help. Are you working on it every day like I told you?"

"Yes, I'm working on it," she said.

"Work your arms more in the last hundred," he said. "When your legs are really tired, you need to use your arms to get you to the finish line."

Kat nodded her head. Then after a moment or two, she said, "I'll get better." She looked up at the coach.

"Good," said the coach. "And don't worry. It'll come." Coach Cox smiled at her.

"Thanks, Coach," said Kat.

Kat told herself to be positive. The coach expected a lot, but he was a really good coach, and he was kind. She was a winner, she told herself, and she was going to get on the team for the Nationals! OK, it was tough right now, but she was used to that. That's the way it was if you wanted to be the best.

Kat started to eat better, went to bed earlier and tried to warm up better before her training sessions. At training, Kat worked even harder. But however hard she tried, Tara Patel and the others were just so much faster and stronger than her.

There was a big competition coming before the Nationals, and Kat noticed that the coach spent more and more time with the girls who were sure to get onto the team. Though he was kind to Kat, it seemed he wanted to work with the others more.

At the following Monday training session, Kat watched them all. "Yes, that's it, Tara!" the coach shouted one time, as Tara Patel went through her exercises. "You're really getting better at that first hundred!" Then he stood talking to Tara and the other girls, giving them some help with their running.

"With the 400, think of the race as four one-hundred meters," he said. "Break it into four; that way it will be easier to manage your energy."

Kat looked at them all as they stood, talking and laughing. Most of them looked as fresh as if it was the beginning of their training, not the end. It was surprising just how strong they were, she thought, and how quickly they were able to recover after a training run. Was it Coach Cox who was helping them to be like this? She remembered the coach's words, "It will come," and she tried to push herself more.

But at the end of the training session, Kat felt disappointed with herself that she just couldn't seem to get any closer to the others' performances. She walked the 200 meters to the changing rooms, her head full of thoughts and worries.

As she got near the building where the changing rooms were, she heard a young woman's voice.

"What's the matter? You look really down."

Kat looked up and saw a girl of about nineteen, with a pleasant, smiling face and lots of brown curly hair.

"Gina," the young woman said. "I run the 800-meters."

"Yes, I think I've seen you around the track." Kat tried to smile, then said, "Hi . . . I'm Kat, Kat Gupta. 400. I'm sorry, I feel a bit . . ."

"Unhappy?"

"Yes, I guess," said Kat.

"Want to talk about it?" Gina asked.

Kat thought the girl looked kind. "Sure," she said.

"We can go for a coffee if you like. I know a good place."

"OK. I'll just be a few minutes!" Kat smiled and ran into the changing room.

Chapter 3

Pizza and a talk

A week later, Kat and Gina were at Napoli pizza restaurant, not far from the track where the club trained. They sometimes trained at the same times and then traveled on the Tube together or went for a pizza at Napoli. It felt good to have a friend in the club at last.

"How are things going?" Gina asked Kat as their pizzas arrived at their table.

Gina started at the club about six months ago, so she was new, too. She was an 800-meter runner, which meant she and Kat weren't competitors. Kat liked her. Gina was open, funny, and friendly.

"Oh, OK," said Kat. She picked up a piece of pizza, and then put it down again without eating. "But I don't think the coach will pick me to go to the National Championships," she said.

"Really?" Gina said. "But there're still over two months to the Nationals . . ."

"I don't know, Gina," Kat said. "I'm just not improving quickly enough."

"You're impatient," Gina said.

Kat took some pizza, and neither of them spoke as she ate it. "Maybe. But I'm just not fast enough," she said finally.

"You will be," said Gina. "It just takes time."

It was quiet for a moment or two. Then, "I'm working really hard," Kat said again. "Much harder than Tara Patel. But I just can't seem to beat her. And if I don't beat her, then I'm not going to be on the team."

"Well, there's still time," Gina said. "Don't be so hard on yourself."

They ate without speaking for a moment or two. Then Kat saw that Gina put her hand in her bag and took out a small box with pills in it. She took a pill out of the box, put it into her mouth quickly, and then drank some water to wash it down.

"Got a headache?" asked Kat.

"Not exactly," said Gina. "I've got a race in a few days and it's just something to help on race day. Want one? They're good for training, too."

Kat shook her head. She looked at her friend like she wanted to ask her a question.

"They're just something to help your performance, Kat, make you feel better," Gina said.

"But are they . . . allowed?"

Gina laughed. "Kat! They're not banned or anything. Everybody takes them."

Kat looked at Gina, not knowing what to say, or even think.

"They could help you," Gina added.

Kat didn't speak.

"Well, whatever," Gina said.

A minute or two later, Gina looked at her watch and said, "Wow! Is that the time?" She quickly ate a piece of pizza, picked up her bag, and stood up.

"Listen, I have to go," she said, putting on her coat. "But I'll see you soon, OK? Bye, Kat."

"Bye."

And with that, Gina walked out of the door of the restaurant. Kat looked at the door, asking herself what that was all about. Then she turned back to her pizza. As she looked down she saw, near Gina's dirty plate, one small pill on the table. *Maybe Gina dropped it from the box,* Kat thought.

Kat picked it up and ran to the door, but the street was dark and Gina was already gone.

Chapter 4

24 hours

Kat sat down at her table. She looked at the pill carefully and touched it with the tip of her finger. What was it? There was no writing on it, nothing to tell her what it was. The only thing on it was a mark, a little circle. *"They're not banned or anything. Everybody takes them."* Kat looked round the restaurant quickly and put it into her pocket.

On the bus and the Tube, Kat couldn't stop thinking about the pill. She thought about it in her pocket.

"Hello, darling," her mother called from the living room as she walked into her house. "How was it today?"

"Oh, OK," Kat replied. "Feel a bit tired, so I think I'll go straight to bed."

She went upstairs to her bedroom. She put the pill into an envelope, then put it into the drawer in the table next to her bed. She got ready for bed. *I'll think about that tomorrow,* she thought.

But when she went to bed, she found it difficult to sleep. She was awake most of the night, thinking about the pill, and thinking about Gina. Then she told herself not to be silly. They were probably something you took just to make you feel less tired. *"They're not banned or anything. Everybody takes them."* She kept hearing Gina's voice.

Early next morning, Kat called Salma and then went over to her house to see her. It was Wednesday and Salma didn't have classes at college until later in the day.

"What's the big secret?" asked Salma, laughing, as she opened the door. Then she saw Kat's serious face. "Come upstairs," she said.

Kat told Salma about Gina and the pill.

"Can I see it?" asked Salma.

Kat took the envelope out of her inside pocket and showed Salma.

"Maybe they're OK," said Kat. "But I need to find out. Gina's a friend of mine and . . ."

"Hmm," said Salma, looking at the pill with a worried face.

They both thought for a moment.

"I know!" said Salma suddenly. "Moin!"

"Moin?" asked Kat.

"Moin works in pharmacy, remember?" said Salma.

"Yes . . . ?"

"Well, I'm sure he can look in a book at the pharmacy and find out what it is," said Salma.

"Good idea!" said Kat.

"I'll get it to Moin and I'll call you later," said Salma.

"Thanks, Salma." Kat hugged her friend and left for college.

Kat waited for Salma's call all day. That evening, Kat found it hard to keep her mind on her training. *What's happened to Salma?* she wondered. *What about the pill? Did Moin find out about them today?*

Then, finally, as she was leaving the training ground, her phone rang. She saw it was Salma's number.

"Salma! Finally," she said. "What is it?"

"I think you need to come here on your way home," Salma said.

Chapter 5

Hard days

"Come into the kitchen," Salma said, as she showed Kat into her house. "Mom and Dad are watching TV in the living room. They won't hear anything," she added.

Kat followed Salma into the kitchen at the back of the house. Moin was waiting there, sitting at the big table. He looked at Kat and said hi, but his smile showed that he was worried.

"It's not good news, Kat," he said.

Kat sat down at the table. "Oh?"

"I've looked in a book for the mark on the pill, the circle." Moin's handsome face looked serious.

"Yes?" asked Kat. "So . . ."

Moin didn't speak immediately. Finally, he said, "It seems to be Ethadren."

"Ethadren?" asked Kat. She said the name in her head once or twice. "It sounds . . ." Kat was sure she'd read the name somewhere.

"It's a kind of stimulant," explained Moin.

"A stimulant . . . I . . ."

"It makes your heart beat faster and your blood pressure go up . . ."

"Oh . . ." Kat started to feel sick in her stomach.

Moin went on. "If athletes take this kind of thing, they can run faster, jump higher, just generally perform better."

"I understand," said Kat. "And it's banned, right?"

Moin nodded his head.

"So it *is* . . . cheating," said Kat.

Salma got up and made tea, and the three of them sat talking.

"Now I remember," Kat said. "I read something about this Ethadren stuff in a magazine. It was an athlete, a 200-meter runner, I think, a girl in Austria. They tested her after a race and found it. She was banned for two years or something . . . I can't remember anything else about it."

"That sounds possible," said Moin. "I mean the ban."

"The thing is," said Kat, "is it just Gina who's taking this, or are the others at the club, too?"

Kat drank the hot tea and tried to think. Was this what was making some of the girls so fast? And when Gina said, "Everybody takes them," was she talking about the other runners at Kingston Harriers? And Gina. She had to know what the pills were, didn't she?

I have to watch what's going on at the club, Kat told herself as she walked home.

For the next few days, Kat tried not to see much of Gina as she decided to find out about the other athletes.

She watched the other girls carefully during training, and in the changing room. Most of them knew each other really well. They were always together, partly because they all lived near Kingston Harriers club. It was clear that they had all known each other a long time. Still, she didn't see them taking any pills, or acting unusually. But she kept thinking of Gina's words, *"Everybody takes them."*

And what about Gina? Maybe even Gina herself didn't know what exactly they were. But then . . . Kat didn't know what to think. Finally, she told herself that she *had* to talk to Gina about it. One evening after training she saw Gina in the changing rooms.

"Want to come for a coffee?" she asked.

"Sure."

They went to the Bad Dog café and sat at a table well away from everyone else. They talked about training for a few minutes. Then Kat said, "Listen, those pills you had the other day at Napoli . . ."

"Yes?" Gina said carefully.

"Well, you dropped one on the table . . ."

Gina looked surprised.

"And . . . well, I asked someone to find out what it is."

"Really?" Gina's face went red.

"I'm sorry. I had to . . ."

Gina didn't speak.

"Gina, I . . . I don't know if you know this, but that stuff is Ethadren. It's a banned stimulant. If you take it and they find it in your body after a race, you're in big trouble. It's cheating."

"I told you, Kat," Gina said. "It's nothing. Everybody takes that stuff. Don't worry about it."

"When you say *everybody*, do you mean the other runners at the club?"

"Some of them . . . Oh, I don't know, Kat," Gina said, getting angry. "Stop questioning me! Who do you think you are? The police or something?"

"Gina, I just don't want to see you . . ." Kat tried to explain.

"What?" Gina said. "It's not your business, Kat."

"But Gina, I . . ."

"What makes *you* so different, anyway?"

"Really, Gina . . ."

"Listen. You're wondering why you're not winning. Maybe this is why. It's because you're not prepared to do what you need to do to be a winner!"

And with that, Gina jumped up and walked out of the café.

Chapter 6

Hard training

Kat told herself that she had done the right thing in talking to Gina and telling her what she knew. Gina wasn't happy about it, but it was up to her now. And the others? She didn't know anything about them. She had no proof that they took Ethadren. If they did take it, she was disappointed, but that was up to them. If they got caught, that was the end for them.

The coach was great and people said the club had more international athletes than any other club in the country, she told herself. Her job was to train as hard as she could and achieve her goals. She wanted to get a time of 52.50. That time gave her at least a chance of getting on the National team.

Now she started to train harder, and to think only about training. *If I want to be the best, I have to get stronger*, she told herself.

She got up earlier in the mornings and ran around the streets near her house before she went to college. When she came back into the house to get ready, it was still only 7:30, and her mother and father were usually just finishing their breakfast and going to work.

"Kat!" her mother said to her. "I'm starting to get worried about you training so hard!"

But Kat just laughed. In the evenings at the club, she stayed on the track longer to do more exercises.

But still, she found she couldn't quite beat Tara Patel's time. Kat was two-hundredths of a second slower.

Kat increased her training even more. She started trying to improve her leg strength with heavier weights. She worked so hard that she got sick and had to take three days off college and off training.

"Be careful, Kat," Coach Cox said. "You're over-training, and you could make yourself very sick."

But soon she was back again, and training just as hard. She thought mainly about beating Tara Patel. Sometimes, now, she thought about the pills. They came into her mind, even when she tried not to think about them. It wasn't natural what these girls could do, she told herself. How did they recover so quickly?

She found herself thinking new thoughts. *What if I did take something, just to give me a bit of help?* she asked herself. She tried to forget about it, but it never went away completely.

One evening after training, the coach talked to Kat's group. "OK, listen, everyone," he said. "As you know, we've got a competition next weekend, against Bexley Athletic Club. It's a really good chance to test ourselves before the Nationals. And I expect us to win." He looked at all the 400-meter runners. First, he called out the names of the boys. Then it was the girls' turn. "Jackie, Pippa, Jane, Tara, I want you to run in the 400-meters individual and the relay."

The coach stopped. Kat felt disappointed that she wouldn't run in the competition. Then he looked at her and continued, "Kat, you'll run the 400-meters individual, too, just so that I can see what you can do in a competition. Thanks, everyone. Good night."

This is my chance, thought Kat as she walked to the changing rooms. *But I have to do well. I have to beat Tara Patel.* Kat was excited. She imagined running well. She saw it in her mind, thought about how it would feel. She walked into the changing rooms and started to get changed.

"Hi, Kat."

Kat turned and saw it was Gina.

"Oh, hi . . ."

"I haven't seen you around much," Gina said.

"No," Kat said. "Training hard . . ." The two of them hadn't talked since the evening at the Bad Dog.

Kat looked at Gina and started to think about the pills again. She tried to put them out of her mind, but she couldn't. Maybe the pills were the difference between Kat and the others. Maybe if she took something, just once, she could be a winner too. And she only had to ask Gina. She knew that Gina would be happy to give some to her. *If everyone's taking them*, thought Kat, *why not me?*

Kat fought with her own thoughts for a few moments.

"Gina, I . . ."

"What?"

"I'm . . ." Kat looked at Gina. Then finally she said, "Oh, nothing."

Gina looked at Kat for a moment or two. "Are you sure you don't want one?" she asked finally.

Kat nodded her head. "Yes," she said.

"OK," said Gina. "It's your choice."

Kat picked up her things and hurried out of the changing rooms.

On the way home, her mind was busy. *Cheat or lose?* she thought, as she looked at the busy streets outside the bus. Was that the choice she had to make as a 400-meter runner? *Everybody takes them.* That's what Gina said. Did this mean that she would lose?

Chapter 7

Competition!

The competition against Bexley Athletic Club was one of the big events of the year for Kingston Harriers. Bexley were great rivals, and Coach Cox always liked to beat them. The National Championships were in two weeks. He liked to take his team there full of confidence.

Kat got through the first rounds of the 400-meters easily and got into the final race. Her times improved in every round. But for the final, she had to line up against all the best runners from her own club as well as Bexley's. She knew it would be hard to even get in the first four. But she told herself that she wanted to run her own personal best time of 52.50. That was her goal. *I only want to run fast if I know it's me*, she told herself. *I don't want to cheat!*

Kat got into line for her race. She couldn't see Tara Patel at all. Where was she? She didn't have time to ask because the race started. From the start, Kat ran as hard as she could. Her start was fast. She ran around the track using her legs to really push her. One hundred meters. Two hundred meters. Three hundred. When she reached the final hundred meters, she saw that Jackie and Pippa, the best runners from Kingston Harriers, were well in front of her. Michelle Mah from Bexley Athletic Club was just in front of her, too. Kat pushed and pushed herself, trying to catch the three girls in front of her. She reached the line just behind them and fell to the ground, exhausted.

"Good run, Kat," said Coach Cox. She had finished fourth, but with a time of 52.50. That was her own personal best time.

"Thanks, Coach," Kat smiled.

After a few minutes, Kat got up and went to the changing rooms. She showered and changed. She was tired, but happy. She knew that that time took her closer toward her goal of getting onto the National Team. She would go back and watch the girls in the 400-meter relay later.

She left the changing room.

"Kat!" Kat turned when she heard her name. It was Coach Cox. There was no one else around; all the athletes were outside on the track, watching the races.

"Yes, Coach?"

"How are you?" he asked. He looked worried, she thought, kind of nervous.

"OK, a bit tired," she said. "Is something wrong?"

"It's Tara," the coach said. "She's got a stomach problem. That's why she didn't run in the individual 400. She can't run in the relay either. I sent her home already. I . . . we need you to run . . ."

"I'm not sure I can," Kat said. "I feel really tired."

"It's your big moment," he said. "If you do this well, you have a great chance of going to the Nationals."

"Really?" she said. "That's great, but honestly, I don't know if I can."

"I know it's a bit unfair asking you to run the race at the last moment, but do your best."

"I don't know . . ." said Kat. "I want to, but I'm a bit worried I'll disappoint you and the team."

The coach smiled kindly. Then he reached into the pocket of his track suit and brought out a small white box. "Look, take this," he said. "It's just something to make you less tired."

Kat's heart jumped, and she looked at the coach. "What's that?" she asked.

"I told you," he said. "It's just something to make you feel less tired. We usually give these to athletes who have injuries."

Kat just looked at Coach Cox.

The coach laughed a little. "Kat? Would I give you anything bad?"

Kat opened the box and found a little white pill. It was exactly the same as the one Gina had dropped on the table in the pizza restaurant.

Kat felt like someone had hit her in the stomach. Now it was all clear. They were cheating, all of them, and it was the coach who was giving them the pills!

She looked at Coach Cox and moved away from him. "No. No way," she said. "I want to win, but not this way." She threw the pill on the floor.

Suddenly, Kat remembered what she had read in the magazine about the Austrian runner and Ethadren. The coach! The girl told the police that her coach gave her the banned stimulant. Then the police went to his house and found that it was full of Ethadren and other stimulants. Now the Austrian coach was in prison for giving banned stimulants to young people.

"But Kat," the coach started. "It's just . . ."

"It's just . . . something that's banned," she said, looking

him in the eye. "It's cheating, Coach, and it's better to lose than cheat."

"Well, now . . ."

Kat looked at Coach Cox angrily. "And all the help you gave me? And you were so kind! Was that so that I would trust you? So I'll take anything from you, even a banned stimulant like Ethadren?"

"Now, Kat . . ."

"You're giving athletes in this club banned stimulants, Coach. But not me!" Kat was so angry that she was almost crying now. She turned and started walking.

"What are you doing?" asked the coach.

But Kat just walked away.

Chapter 8

The Nationals

A few weeks later, Kat waited for the start of the 400-meter final. She was at the National Championships in Manchester, and she was wearing the blue and gold colors of Bexley Athletic. Bexley may not be as "good" as Kingston Harriers, she thought, but the coach and the runners weren't cheats. She was nervous and took a few deep breaths. She looked up into the big crowd. Her parents were up there, and Salma and Moin, too.

Kat had to be in the top three to have a chance of being chosen for the Great Britain team. She looked down the line of young women ready to run. Jackie, Jane, Pippa, and Tara were there, running the 400 for Kingston Harriers. Tara Patel was right next to Kat, but they didn't speak. Kat knew that Coach Cox was around somewhere, too. She just hoped not to see him.

As soon as Kat thought about Coach Cox, she thought about the conversation she had with Salma after he'd offered her banned stimulants.

"Are you going to tell the police?" Salma said.

"No," Kat said. "No, I'm not. I'm just going to show I can win without cheating."

Salma looked at her friend.

"And if I don't win and get on the Great Britain team," Kat added, "I'm going to try something else, Salma. I'm going to leave the 400. I want to do something where I can succeed without cheating!"

Now she looked in front of her at the track.

The race began. Kat started well. For the first hundred she was just in front of Tara Patel. They were both just behind Jackie, Jane, and Pippa. Then in the second hundred, Tara moved a little in front of Kat. Kat breathed deeply and pushed hard. She started to move in front again, so that in the third hundred, she was ahead of Tara. Then, at the end of the third hundred, Jackie stopped running. She moved off the track, holding her leg. She was injured!

Now's my chance, thought Kat. *If only I can beat Tara! If only I can get in the top three!*

Pippa and Jane were now just in front. Then came Tara and Kat. Kat pushed and pushed and pushed. Her legs started to burn, but she pushed on. In the fourth hundred she was in front of Tara, then behind, then in front again. Finally, Tara Patel moved in front, beating Kat into third place by just one-hundredth of a second.

Kat fell exhausted to the ground. She looked up quickly to see the times. Hers was a new personal best of 52.20!

"A personal best, that's wonderful," her mother said. Mrs. Gupta hugged her daughter.

"Fantastic!" the others agreed.

"Yeah, I guess so," said Kat, smiling. *Well, that's that*, Kat thought as she went off to be tested. *Time to try something else.* But she'd done her best, she knew, and she had no regrets about anything.

After Kat's test, she, her mom and dad, and Salma and Moin started to leave the grounds where the Nationals were held. They walked past Pippa, wearing her winner's medal, and Jane and Tara. They were in a group with the others from Kingston Harriers, and Coach Cox was there too, Kat saw. He turned when he saw Kat. He looked like he wanted to talk to her, but Kat looked away.

Three days later, Kat was at home when she got a telephone call.

"Miss Gupta?"

"Yes?"

It was one of the race officials from the Nationals. "Can you come to the Nationals office here in London, please?" the official said. "There's been a change in your race results from the other day."

"Change?"

"Yes," said the man. "But you'll have to come to see the chief race official. She'll tell you everything."

Kat called Salma, and later they went down to the office in central London.

"Two of the girls who were ahead of you," said the chief official, a woman of about forty with a lot of red hair, "their names are Jane Howe and Tara Patel . . . ?"

"Yes?"

"Well, we tested them, like we tested you," said the official, "and it seems they took something to improve their performance."

Kat looked at the woman.

"A banned stimulant called Ethadren," said the chief official, shaking her head. "It looks like their coach gave it to them. This is not good for them, or for the coach."

"What will happen to Jane, Tara, and Coach Cox?" Kat asked

"Well, the coach will be banned," said the official.

"Maybe even put in prison. He's coming here later. One thing is sure—he'll never coach again." The official shook her head.

"So . . . ?"

"So you came in second. Congratulations!"

This is like a dream, thought Kat.

Just then a woman with short blonde hair walked up to Kat and Salma. "Kat Gupta?" The woman was smiling.

"That's me," said Kat.

"I'm Mary King," the woman said.

Kat looked at the woman. "Aren't you . . . ?" she started.

"The Great Britain Women's National Coach," the woman said. "And the thing is, Kat, you came in second with a great time of 52.20 and I'd like to invite you to come and train with the Great Britain team."

Kat just looked at the woman. She couldn't speak. *Now this is really like a dream!* she thought.

"Well done!" Mary King added.

"That's great, Kat," said Salma. She hugged her friend.

Kat still had no words for a minute or two. Finally, she said, "Thanks, I'm . . . well . . . really happy."

For the next twenty minutes, Kat talked to Mary King about the training times for the Great Britain team. Then Kat and Salma walked toward the door, laughing and talking as they went. As they walked through the door, they almost fell into someone who was coming into the office. Kat looked up. It was Coach Cox. And he was walking in with a policeman.

Kat looked at the coach and caught his eye. For a moment they looked at each other.

"Come on," said Salma, taking Kat's arm. "Let's go home and celebrate."

"Yes," said Kat, turning away from the coach and smiling. "Let's go and celebrate!"

Review: Chapters 1–4

A. **Match the characters in the story to their descriptions. Two answers are extra.**

Kat	Salma	Moin	Tara Patel	Coach Cox	Gina

1. _____ is an 18-year-old 400-meter runner who has just changed clubs.

2. _____ is the second slowest of the five girls who run the 400 meters at Kingston Harriers.

3. _____ loves history.

4. _____ works at a pharmacy.

B. **Number these events in the order they happened (1–6).**

_____ Kat and Gina go to the pizza restaurant.

_____ Gina takes a pill.

_____ Salma suggests that Moin helps.

_____ Gina leaves a pill on the table.

_____ Kat and Salma talk about the pill in Salma's bedroom.

_____ Kat meets Gina for the first time outside the changing rooms.

C. **Read each statement and circle whether it is true (T) or false (F).**

1. Kat is the second-fastest runner in the 400 meters at Kingston Harriers.   T / F

2. Salma studies Sports Science.   T / F

3. Kat won a big competition when she was 10 years old.   T / F

4. When Kat and Gina first meet, they go for a coffee together.   T / F

5. When Kat sees Gina taking a pill, she feels it is wrong.   T / F

Review: Chapters 5–8

A. Complete the summary with the correct word from the box.

stimulant	business	goals	pill	club	athletes

When Kat finds out that the **1.** _____ that Gina left behind
in the restaurant is a **2.** _____, she decides to watch what is
going on at the **3.** _____. She talks to Gina, but Gina tells Kat
that it's not her **4.** _____. Kat doesn't notice any of the other
5. _____ taking anything bad. Kat decides to think about her own
training, and to try to achieve her **6.** _____ .

B. Who said this? Choose the correct answer from the box. One name is extra.

Gina	Coach Cox	Moin	Mrs. Gupta	Kat

1. "It makes your heart beat faster and your blood
pressure go up . . ."   _____

2. "It's because you're not prepared to do what you
need to do to be a winner!"   _____

3. "You're over-training, and you could make yourself
very sick."   _____

4. "I want to do something where I can succeed
without cheating!"   _____

C. **Choose the best answer for each question.**

1. In the individual 400-meter race against Bexley Athletic, Kat _____.

   a. runs a personal best   c. beats Tara Patel

   b. wins   d. falls

2. The coach wants Kat to run the relay against Bexley Athletic because _____.

   a. Pippa has a cold

   b. Kat begs him to let her run

   c. Jackie's leg is injured

   d. Tara has a stomach problem

3. Kat throws away the pill Coach Cox gives her before the competition against Bexley Athletic because _____.

   a. she doesn't think the pill will work

   b. she doesn't want to cheat

   c. she is not sick

   d. her friend Salma advised her to do it

4. The National Championships take place _____.

   a. in London   c. in Hull

   b. in Manchester   d. in Birmingham

5. At the National Championships, Kat is _____.

   a. running for Kingston Harriers

   b. running for Bexley Athletic

   c. running with Salma

   d. not running

6. After the National Championships, Kat is invited _____.

   a. by Coach Cox to train with Kingston Harriers again

   b. by Coach Johnson to train with Bexley Athletic

   c. by Mary King to train with the Great Britain team

   d. by the national coach of France to train in France

Answer Key

Chapters 1–4

A:
1. Kat; **2.** Tara Patel; **3.** Salma; **4.** Moin

B:
2, 3, 6, 4, 5, 1

C:
1. F; **2.** F; **3.** T; **4.** T; **5.** T

Chapters 5–8

A:
1. pill; **2.** stimulant; **3.** club; **4.** business; **5.** athletes; **6.** goals

B:
1. Moin; **2.** Gina; **3.** Coach Cox; **4.** Kat

C:
1. b; **2.** a; **3.** d; **4.** b; **5.** b; **6.** c

Background Reading:
Spotlight on . . . *Drugs in sport*

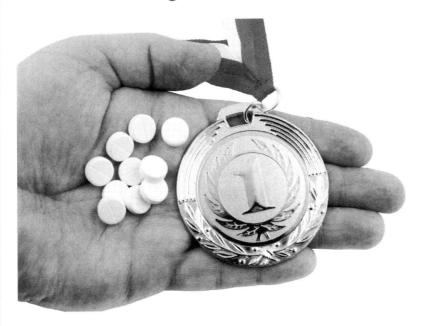

Creatine?[1] Anabolic steroids?[2] Have you heard of them? Do you know that taking these drugs can be dangerous for your health? Some teenage athletes take these performance-enhancing drugs to improve their results. But many don't realize the dangers of these drugs. Also, if you are caught taking these drugs by sports officials, you can be disqualified from your sport. And it is possible that you will not be able to compete again in that sport.

There are many dangers of taking drugs to improve your performance in sport. Physically, you are doing harm to your body: the liver and the kidney can be damaged. Your appearance can also change—your face can become swollen and rounded, and acne can appear. You also gain weight. Users of anabolic steroids also find that their bone growth stops, so they don't grow taller.

What are some of the factors that lead teenagers to use these drugs? As the drugs help you put on muscle mass, boys rather than girls are more likely to use them to gain weight. Other reasons may be pressure from friends regarding weight or muscles. Some young adults think that taking drugs would make them popular with their friends who are also taking them.

A famous case of drug use in sport is that of Lance Armstrong. Armstrong is a former professional road cyclist who won the Tour de France seven times between 1999 and 2005. He was later discovered to have been using drugs. Because of this, he was disqualified and banned from cycling for life by the United States Anti-Doping Agency (USADA) in 2012. Armstrong's case reminds us that we should not use drugs no matter how much we want to win.

Think About It

1. What do you think is the best way to warn young people about the dangers of performance-enhancing drugs?
2. Do you think young athletes who cheat should be banned from their sport? Or should they get a second chance?

[1]**Creatine** is a drug that helps build muscle mass and strength.

[2]**Anabolic steroids** are like the hormone testosterone. They build muscles and increase strength. Some side effects are heart and liver damage, and bone growth is stopped so teenagers stay short.

Glossary

athlete	(*n.*)	sportsman or sportswoman
banned	(*adj.*)	not allowed
celebrate	(*v.*)	to have a party
champion	(*n.*)	winner of a competition
cheat	(*v.*)	to go against the rules
club	(*n.*)	a group of people organized for a purpose, e.g., athletic club
disappointed	(*adj.*)	sad because something was not as good as expected
gym	(*n.*)	(gymnasium) a building or room designed and equipped for indoor sports, exercise, or physical education
hug	(*v.*)	to hold someone closely
performance	(*n.*)	the act of doing something; something accomplished
pharmacy	(*n.*)	a place where you buy medicine
proof	(*n.*)	evidence that shows that something is true
race	(*n.*)	a competition of speed, e.g., running
relay	(*n.*)	a kind of race with four runners running as a team
stimulant	(*n.*)	a drug that makes athletes faster
track	(*n.*)	the ground where a runner runs
Tube	(*n.*)	the underground train in London